States CALIFORNIA

by Jason Kirchner

CAPSTONE PRESS
a capstone imprint

Next Page Books are published by Capstone Press,
1710 Roe Crest Drive, North Mankato, Minnesota 56003
www.mycapstone.com

Library of Congress Cataloging-in-Publication Data
Cataloging-in-publication information is on file with the Library of
Congress.
ISBN 978-1-5157-0391-4 (library binding)
ISBN 978-1-5157-0451-5 (paperback)
ISBN 978-1-5157-0503-1 (ebook PDF)

Editorial Credits
Jaclyn Jaycox, editor; Katelin Plekkenpol and Katy LaVigne, designers;
Morgan Walters, media researcher; Laura Manthe, production specialist

Photo Credits
Capstone Press: Angi Gahler, map 4, 7; CriaImages.com: Jay Robert
Nash Collection, bottom 18, middle 19, bottom 19, top left 21, middle
18; Dreamstime: Igor Boldyrev, middle left 21, Twildlife, 21; Getty
Images: Stock Montage, 25; Library of Congress: Library of Congress
Prints and Photographs Division Washington, D.C., 28; Newscom:
Ed Rhodes/TTL/Photoshot, 9; One Mile Up, Inc: (seal, flag) 22-23;
Shutterstock: Africa Studio, bottom right 21, Alan C. Heison, top
19, Andrew Zarivny, 5, ChameleonsEye, 17, dean bertoncelj, bottom
24, Everett Historical, 12, 27, Featureflash, top 18, Felix Lipov, 11,
iofoto, top left 20, Jan-Dirk Hansen, bottom right 20, top right 21,
jessicakirsh, cover, Jose Gil, 26, littleny, 6, Lorcel, 7, N. F. Photography,
29, Oreena, bottom left 21, Pal Teravagimov, top 24, Rada Photos, 13,
Roka, 10, Stas Volik, bottom right 8, stefbennett, 14, Thomas Barrat,
15, Tom Reichner, bottom left 20, View Apart, 16, Vladimir Sazonov, top
right 20, welcomia, bottom left 8

All design elements by Shutterstock

Printed and bound in China.
0316/CA21600187
012016   009436F16

TABLE OF CONTENTS

Want to take your research further? Ask your librarian if your school subscribes to PebbleGo Next. If so, when you see this helpful symbol ⊕ throughout the book, log onto www.pebblegonext.com for bonus downloads and information.

LOCATION

California is located on the western edge of the United States. California is the third-largest state in the country. Its long coast faces the Pacific Ocean. Oregon lies north of California. To the south is Mexico. Nevada and Arizona are on the east. Sacramento is the capital of California. It is in north-central California. California's biggest cities are Los Angeles, San Diego, San Jose, and San Francisco.

PebbleGo Next Bonus! To print and label your own map, go to www.pebblegonext.com and search keywords:

CA MAP

OREGON

IDAHO

N
W E
S

•Eureka
•Redding
•Chico

Lake Tahoe

PACIFIC OCEAN

Sacramento ✪

NEVADA

UTAH

•Stockton
San Francisco•
•Oakland
•San Jose

•Fresno

CALIFORNIA

Bakersfield•

ARIZONA

Legend
✪ Capital
• City
◠ Lake
〰 River

Santa Barbara•

•Los Angeles
•San Bernadino
•Palm Springs

Colorado River

•San Diego

Scale
Miles
0 40 80 120 160
0 40 80 120 160
Kilometers

MEXICO

4

There are about 1,475,000 people living in Sacramento, California's capital.

GEOGRAPHY

California is a state with many land features. Coastlands and islands form California's western border. Mountains, valleys, and deserts fill out the rest of the state. Forests cover California's northern coastline. The Cascades are California's northernmost mountains. A mountain range called the Sierra Nevada lies along California's border with Nevada. Mount Whitney in the southern part of the Sierra Nevada is the state's highest point. It is 14,495 feet (4,418 meters) high. Lake Tahoe lies on the northern part of the California-Nevada border. It is the largest mountain lake in North America. The Mojave Desert lies in southern California.

PebbleGo Next Bonus!
To watch a video about
Yosemite National Park, go
to www.pebblegonext.com
and search keywords:
CA VIDEO

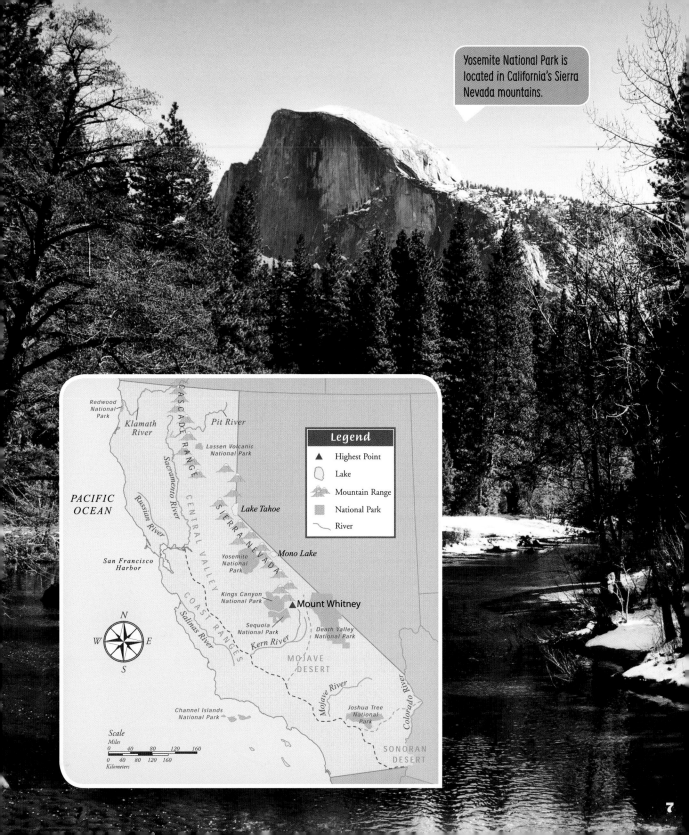

Yosemite National Park is located in California's Sierra Nevada mountains.

Legend
- ▲ Highest Point
- Lake
- Mountain Range
- National Park
- River

PACIFIC OCEAN

Redwood National Park

Klamath River

Pit River

CASCADE RANGE

Lassen Volcanic National Park

Sacramento River

Russian River

CENTRAL VALLEY

SIERRA NEVADA

Lake Tahoe

Mono Lake

Yosemite National Park

Kings Canyon National Park

▲ Mount Whitney

San Francisco Harbor

COAST RANGES

Salinas River

Sequoia National Park

Kern River

Death Valley National Park

MOJAVE DESERT

Mojave River

Colorado River

Channel Islands National Park

Joshua Tree National Park

SONORAN DESERT

Scale
Miles
0   40   80   120   160
0   40   80   120   160
Kilometers

N W E S

WEATHER

California has a warm climate. The average summer temperature is 73 degrees Fahrenheit (23 degrees Celsius). The average winter temperature is 46°F (8°C).

Average High and Low Temperatures (Sacramento, CA)

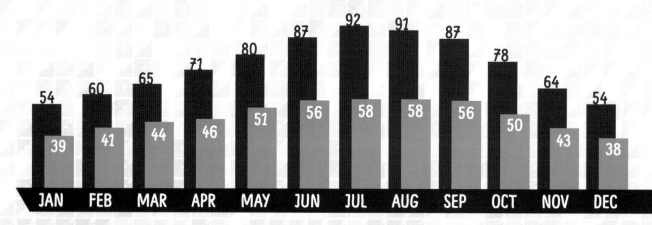

	JAN	FEB	MAR	APR	MAY	JUN	JUL	AUG	SEP	OCT	NOV	DEC
High	54	60	65	71	80	87	92	91	87	78	64	54
Low	39	41	44	46	51	56	58	58	56	50	43	38

LANDMARKS

Disneyland

Disneyland is a massive amusement park and resort in Anaheim. Disneyland has entertained more than 650 million people since it opened in 1955. Visitors can get their pictures taken with their favorite Disney characters.

SeaWorld

SeaWorld in San Diego is one of the most popular marine parks in the world. More than 155 million people have visited SeaWorld since it opened in 1964. Visitors enjoy dolphin and whale shows, aquariums, rides, and educational programs.

Sequoia National Park

Sequoia National Park in the Sierra Nevada has thousands of giant sequoia trees. The park is home to a tree called General Sherman, which is the world's largest tree in volume of wood. Its trunk is more than 102 feet (31 m) around at its base. The tree is about 275 feet (84 m) high. It is between 2,200 and 2,500 years old.

The gold rush brought about 300,000 gold-seekers to California

American Indians lived in California for thousands of years before white people came to the area. The first European in California was explorer Juan Rodriguez Cabrillo in 1542. In 1769 Father Junipero Serra of Spain set up a mission at San Diego. This was the first Spanish settlement in California. In 1822 California became part of Mexico. Then in 1848 the United States won the Mexican War (1846–1848). California then became a U.S. territory. Gold was discovered in northern California in 1848. Within a year, people from around the world came to California looking for gold. In 1850 California became the 31st state.

California's state government has three branches. The governor leads the executive branch. The legislature is made up of the 40-member Senate and the 80-member Assembly. California's judges and courts are the judicial branch. They uphold the laws.

California's state capitol building is located in Sacramento. It also serves as a museum.

INDUSTRY

California is the nation's top agricultural producer. Grapes and milk are among its top farm products. Farmers in California also grow almonds, cotton, avocados, olives, and prunes. California has more dairy cattle than any other state.

More than 80 percent of the state's workers hold jobs in service industries, including tourism and the movie industry. Tourists travel to southern California to visit Disneyland, SeaWorld, and the San Diego Zoo.

California ranks first in the nation in manufacturing. The state produces airplanes, computers, missiles, and chemicals.

A California dairy cow produces an average of almost 24,000 pounds (10,890 kilograms) of milk per year.

Mining is also an important part of California's economy. California is the third-largest gold producer in the country. The state also drills some of its own oil.

California vineyards are known for producing grapes. In fact, they are one of the state's top farming industries.

POPULATION

California has a diverse population. Together California's minority groups make up the largest minority population of any other state. More than one-fourth of the people in California are Hispanic. Large numbers of Mexicans have been coming to California for more than 50 years. Other Hispanic groups include immigrants from Central America and South America. Asians are the third-largest group in California, behind whites and Hispanics. Today about 5 million Asians live in California.

Population by Ethnicity

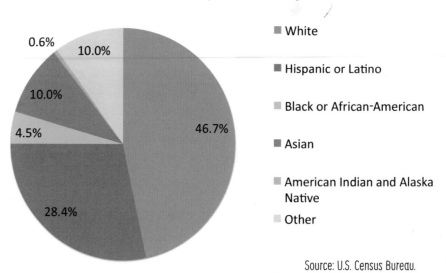

0.6%
10.0%
10.0%
4.5%
46.7%
28.4%

- White
- Hispanic or Latino
- Black or African-American
- Asian
- American Indian and Alaska Native
- Other

Source: U.S. Census Bureau.

FAMOUS PEOPLE

Leonardo DiCaprio (1974–) is an award-winning actor. He has starred in many movies, including *What's Eating Gilbert Grape?* (1993), *Titanic* (1997), *Gangs of New York* (2002), *Inception* (2010), and *The Wolf of Wall Street* (2013). He was born in Los Angeles.

Joe DiMaggio (1914–1999) was a baseball star with the New York Yankees. A powerful batter, he hit 361 home runs in his lifetime. He was born in Martinez.

Richard Nixon (1913–1994) was the 37th president of the United States (1969–1974). Before becoming president, he was vice president under President Dwight Eisenhower (1953–1961). Nixon resigned as president during the Watergate scandal. He was the first U.S. president to resign his office. He was born in Yorba Linda.

Sally Ride (1951–2012) became the first American woman in space in 1983. She was an astronaut from 1979 to 1987 and helped design the robot arm for the space shuttle. She was born in Encino.

William Randolph Hearst (1863–1951) owned dozens of newspapers across the country. He was known for "yellow journalism"—using shocking stories to sell more papers. His elaborate home in San Simeon is called Hearst Castle. He was born in San Francisco.

Junipero Serra (1713–1784) built California's first missions, which were religious centers. Born in Spain, he was a Roman Catholic missionary in the Franciscan order. He sailed to Mexico in 1749. In 1769 he set up the San Diego Mission.

STATE SYMBOLS

Tree

California redwood

Flower

golden poppy

Bird

California valley quail

Reptile

desert tortoise

PebbleGo Next Bonus! To make a dessert with one of California's largest crops, go to www.pebblegonext.com and search keywords: **CA RECIPE**

Fossil

saber-toothed cat

Marine Mammal

California gray whale

Mammal

California grizzly bear

Fish

golden trout

Rock

serpentine

Mineral

gold

FAST FACTS

STATEHOOD
1850

CAPITAL ☆
Sacramento

LARGEST CITY •
Los Angeles

SIZE
155,779 square miles (403,466 square kilometers) land area (2010 U.S. Census Bureau)

POPULATION
38,332,521 (2013 U.S. Census estimate)

STATE NICKNAME
Golden State

STATE MOTTO
"Eureka!," which is Greek for "I have found it!"

PebbleGo Next Bonus!
To learn the lyrics to the state song, go to www.pebblegonext.com and search keywords:
CA SONG

STATE SEAL

California's state seal was adopted in 1849. The woman on the seal is Minerva, the ancient Roman goddess of wisdom. The grizzly bear at her feet represents California's wildlife. The miner in the distance is a symbol of California's gold mining history. In the background is the Sacramento River. Ships on the river stand for California's trade. The word "Eureka" at the top of the seal stands for the discovery of gold.

PebbleGo Next Bonus!
To print and color
your own flag, go to
www.pebblegonext.com
and search keywords:

CA FLAG

STATE FLAG

California's state flag was adopted in 1911. The flag is called the Bear Flag. It is based on the flag raised in the Bear Flag Revolt of 1846 when American settlers in California fought against Mexico's government. The bear is a symbol of strength. It stands for the many grizzly bears that once lived in California. The star is based on the "lone star" of the Texas flag. Underneath the bear are the words "California Republic." A red stripe runs across the bottom of the flag.

MINING PRODUCTS

petroleum, natural gas, sand and gravel, boron minerals

MANUFACTURED GOODS

computer and electronic equipment, petroleum and coal products, chemicals, food products, transportation equipment, fabricated metal products, machinery, plastics and rubber products, clothing

FARM PRODUCTS

beef cattle, vegetables, fruits, nuts, milk, eggs, cotton, greenhouse and nursery products

PROFESSIONAL SPORTS TEAMS

LA Avengers (AFL)
San Jose SaberCats (AFL)
Anaheim Angels (MLB)
Los Angeles Dodgers (MLB)
Oakland Athletics (MLB)
San Diego Padres (MLB)
San Francisco Giants (MLB)
LA Galaxy (MLS)
San Jose Earthquakes (MLS)
Golden State Warriors (NBA)
LA Clippers (NBA)
LA Lakers (NBA)
Sacramento Kings (NBA)
LA Sparks (WNBA)
Sacramento Monarchs (WNBA)
Oakland Raiders (NFL)
San Diego Chargers (NFL)
San Francisco 49'ers (NFL)
Anaheim Mighty Ducks (NHL)
LA Kings (NHL)
San Jose Sharks (NHL)

CALIFORNIA TIMELINE

1542 Explorer Juan Rodríguez Cabrillo sails from Mexico to southern California.

1579 English explorer Francis Drake arrives in California. He claims part of California for England.

1620 The Pilgrims establish a colony in the New World in present-day Massachusetts.

1769 Father Junipero Serra of Spain sets up the first mission at San Diego.

1776 Spanish settlers from Mexico reach San Francisco.

1783 The American colonies win independence from Great Britain in the Revolutionary War (1775–1783).

1822 California, a Spanish territory, becomes part of Mexico after Mexico wins its independence from Spain.

1848 Gold is discovered at Sutter's Mill in northern California; Mexico gives California to the United States after the United States wins the Mexican War (1846–1848).

1849   The Gold Rush begins. People from around the world rush to California to look for gold.

1850   California becomes the 31st state on September 9.

1861–1865   The Union and the Confederacy fight the Civil War. About 17,000 soldiers from California fight for the Union.

1906   A huge earthquake destroys much of San Francisco, killing more than 3,000 people.

1914–1918   World War I is fought; the United States enters the war in 1917.

1937

San Francisco's Golden Gate Bridge opens. The bridge connects northern California to the San Francisco Peninsula.

1939–1945

World War II is fought; the United States enters the war in 1941.

1955

Disneyland opens in Anaheim, which is located about 25 miles (40 km) southeast of Los Angeles.

1962

California passes New York to become the state with the largest population.

1994

An earthquake hits Los Angeles, killing more than 50 people and causing billions of dollars in damages.

2000

Californians suffer a shortage of electricity across the state, as homes and businesses need more electricity than the state's power plants are able to produce.

2003

Voters in California vote to remove Governor Gray Davis from office. Voters elect actor and former professional bodybuilder Arnold Schwarzenegger as governor.

2013

A wildfire called the Rim Fire burns in and near the Stanislaus National Forest in east-central California in the Sierra Nevada. It is California's third-largest wildfire.

2015

Construction begins on the California High Speed Rail System that will connect Los Angeles and San Francisco, which is estimated to cost $68 billion.

Glossary

diverse *(dye-vurss)*—varied or assorted

executive *(ig-ZE-kyuh-tiv)*—the branch of government that makes sure laws are followed

immigrant *(IM-uh-gruhnt)*—someone who comes from one country to live permanently in another country

industry *(IN-duh-stree)*—a business which produces a product or provides a service

legislature *(LEJ-iss-lay-chur)*—a group of elected officials who have the power to make or change laws for a country or state

marine *(muh-REEN)*—to do with the sea

massive *(MASS-iv)*—large, heavy, and solid

minority *(mye-NOR-uh-tee)*—a group that makes up less than half of a large group

mission *(MISH-uhn)*—a church or other place where missionaries live and work

petroleum *(puh-TROH-lee-uhm)*—an oily liquid found below the earth's surface used to make gasoline, heating oil, and many other products

resign *(ri-ZINE)*—to give up a job or position voluntarily

scandal *(SKAN-duhl)*—a dishonest or immoral act that shocks people and disgraces those involved

Read More

Burgan, Michael. *California*. It's My State! New York: Cavendish Square Publishing, 2014.

Ganeri, Anita. *United States of America: A Benjamin Blog and His Inquisitive Dog Guide*. Country Guides. Chicago: Heinemann Raintree, 2015.

Yasuda, Anita. *What's Great About California?* Our Great States. Minneapolis: Lerner Publications, 2015.

Internet Sites

FactHound offers a safe, fun way to find Internet sites related to this book. All of the sites on FactHound have been researched by our staff.

Here's all you do:

Visit *www.facthound.com*

Type in this code: 9781515703914

Check out projects, games and lots more at
www.capstonekids.com

Critical Thinking Using the Common Core

1. California has many well-known landmarks. Can you name three of them? (Key Ideas and Details)

2. In 1962 California passed New York to become the state with the largest population. What are some advantages of living in a state with a large population? What are some disadvantages? (Integration of Knowledge and Ideas)

3. California has the largest minority population of any other state in the United States. What is the definition of minority? Hint: Use your glossary for help! (Craft and Structure)

Index